50 Spicy Southern BBQ Recipes

By: Kelly Johnson

Table of Contents

- Spicy BBQ Pulled Pork Sandwiches
- Hot and Spicy BBQ Chicken Wings
- Cajun BBQ Shrimp Skewers
- Spicy BBQ Brisket
- Carolina Reaper BBQ Ribs
- Nashville Hot Chicken Tenders
- Spicy Smoked Sausage
- Chipotle Honey BBQ Chicken
- Fiery BBQ Shrimp Boil
- Spicy Dry Rub Baby Back Ribs
- Jalapeño BBQ Baked Beans
- Spicy BBQ Meatballs
- Habanero BBQ Pulled Chicken
- Spicy Peach BBQ Pork Chops
- Southern Spicy BBQ Mac and Cheese
- Hot BBQ Burnt Ends
- Spicy Smoked Turkey Legs
- Cajun BBQ Catfish
- Spicy BBQ Beef Short Ribs
- Sweet and Spicy BBQ Cornbread
- Smoked Chicken with Spicy Rub
- Spicy BBQ Pork Belly Bites
- Ghost Pepper BBQ Sauce
- Spicy Blackened Shrimp Tacos
- Fiery BBQ Beef Burgers
- Spicy Grilled Corn with Cajun Butter
- Jalapeño Cheddar BBQ Sausages
- BBQ Brisket Nachos with Spicy Queso
- Carolina Hot Mustard BBQ Sauce
- Spicy BBQ Pulled Beef
- Smoked Hot Link Sausages
- Spicy BBQ Pork Ribs with Bourbon Glaze
- Sweet Heat BBQ Chicken Drumsticks
- BBQ Spicy Pickle Slaw
- Smoked Brisket Chili with BBQ Sauce

- Spicy BBQ Meatloaf
- Southern Spicy BBQ Deviled Eggs
- Habanero Honey BBQ Glazed Salmon
- BBQ Cajun Shrimp and Grits
- Spicy BBQ Lamb Chops
- Spicy Grilled Sweet Potatoes
- BBQ Pulled Pork Jalapeño Poppers
- Spicy BBQ Ribeye Steak
- Firecracker BBQ Sauce
- Smoky Chipotle BBQ Chicken Thighs
- Spicy BBQ Bacon-Wrapped Jalapeños
- Louisiana Spicy BBQ Shrimp
- BBQ Chili-Lime Chicken Skewers
- Hot BBQ Baked Beans with Andouille
- Spicy BBQ Pimento Cheese Dip

Spicy BBQ Pulled Pork Sandwiches

Ingredients:

- 2 lbs pork shoulder
- 1 tablespoon olive oil
- 1 cup onion, finely chopped
- 3 cloves garlic, minced
- 1 cup BBQ sauce
- 2 tablespoons apple cider vinegar
- 1 tablespoon brown sugar
- 1 teaspoon smoked paprika
- 1/2 teaspoon cayenne pepper
- 1/2 teaspoon chili powder
- 1 teaspoon ground cumin
- Salt and pepper to taste
- 4 sandwich buns
- Coleslaw (optional)

Instructions:

1. Heat olive oil in a large skillet over medium heat. Season the pork shoulder with salt and pepper. Sear the pork on all sides until browned, about 4-5 minutes per side. Remove from skillet and set aside.
2. In the same skillet, add chopped onion and garlic. Cook until softened, about 2 minutes. Stir in the BBQ sauce, apple cider vinegar, brown sugar, paprika, cayenne pepper, chili powder, cumin, and a pinch of salt and pepper.
3. Place the seared pork shoulder in a slow cooker or Instant Pot. Pour the BBQ sauce mixture over the pork, ensuring it is well-coated. Cover and cook on low for 8 hours in the slow cooker, or for 60-75 minutes in an Instant Pot on high pressure.
4. Once the pork is tender, shred the meat using two forks. Stir the shredded pork in the sauce until well combined.
5. Toast the sandwich buns in a skillet or oven until golden brown. Spoon the pulled pork onto the bottom half of each bun. Top with coleslaw, if desired, and close the sandwich with the top bun.
6. Serve hot and enjoy your spicy BBQ pulled pork sandwiches!

Hot and Spicy BBQ Chicken Wings

Ingredients:

- 12 chicken wings
- 2 tablespoons olive oil
- 1 teaspoon garlic powder
- 1 teaspoon smoked paprika
- 1/2 teaspoon cayenne pepper
- 1 teaspoon ground black pepper
- 1/2 teaspoon salt
- 1 cup BBQ sauce
- 1 tablespoon hot sauce (optional, for extra heat)

Instructions:

1. Preheat your oven to 400°F (200°C). Line a baking sheet with parchment paper or aluminum foil.
2. In a small bowl, mix olive oil, garlic powder, smoked paprika, cayenne pepper, black pepper, and salt.
3. Toss the chicken wings in the seasoning mixture until evenly coated. Spread the wings in a single layer on the prepared baking sheet.
4. Bake for 25-30 minutes, flipping halfway through, until the wings are crispy and fully cooked.
5. While the wings bake, heat BBQ sauce and hot sauce in a small saucepan over low heat.
6. Once the wings are done, toss them in the sauce until well-coated. Serve hot.

Cajun BBQ Shrimp Skewers

Ingredients:

- 1 lb large shrimp, peeled and deveined
- 2 tablespoons olive oil
- 1 tablespoon Cajun seasoning
- 1 teaspoon garlic powder
- 1/2 teaspoon smoked paprika
- 1/2 teaspoon ground black pepper
- 1 tablespoon lemon juice
- Wooden or metal skewers

Instructions:

1. Preheat your grill to medium-high heat.
2. In a bowl, combine olive oil, Cajun seasoning, garlic powder, paprika, black pepper, and lemon juice.
3. Thread the shrimp onto the skewers. Brush the shrimp with the seasoning mixture.
4. Grill the shrimp for 2-3 minutes per side, or until pink and cooked through.
5. Remove from skewers and serve immediately with extra lemon wedges.

Spicy BBQ Brisket

Ingredients:

- 3-4 lb beef brisket
- 2 tablespoons olive oil
- 1 tablespoon chili powder
- 1 teaspoon cumin
- 1 teaspoon paprika
- 1/2 teaspoon cayenne pepper
- Salt and pepper to taste
- 1 cup BBQ sauce
- 2 tablespoons hot sauce (optional, for extra heat)

Instructions:

1. Preheat your oven to 325°F (163°C).
2. Rub the brisket with olive oil, chili powder, cumin, paprika, cayenne pepper, salt, and pepper.
3. Place the brisket in a roasting pan and cover tightly with aluminum foil. Roast for 3-4 hours, until tender.
4. During the last 30 minutes, mix BBQ sauce with hot sauce (if using) and brush it over the brisket. Return to the oven uncovered for the final cook.
5. Remove from the oven and let it rest for 10 minutes before slicing against the grain. Serve with extra BBQ sauce on the side.

Carolina Reaper BBQ Ribs

Ingredients:

- 2 racks baby back ribs
- 2 tablespoons olive oil
- 1 tablespoon garlic powder
- 1 teaspoon onion powder
- 1 teaspoon smoked paprika
- 1/2 teaspoon ground black pepper
- 1/2 teaspoon salt
- 1 tablespoon brown sugar
- 1 tablespoon Carolina Reaper chili powder (or adjust to taste)
- 1 cup BBQ sauce
- 1 tablespoon apple cider vinegar

Instructions:

1. Preheat your grill or smoker to 275°F (135°C).
2. Remove the membrane from the ribs and pat them dry with a paper towel.
3. Mix olive oil, garlic powder, onion powder, paprika, black pepper, salt, brown sugar, and Carolina Reaper chili powder in a small bowl.
4. Rub the spice mixture generously onto the ribs.
5. Place the ribs on the grill or smoker, bone side down. Cook for 3-4 hours, maintaining a consistent temperature.
6. In the last 30 minutes, brush BBQ sauce mixed with apple cider vinegar onto the ribs for added flavor and moisture.
7. Remove from heat, slice, and serve.

Nashville Hot Chicken Tenders

Ingredients:

- 1 lb chicken tenders
- 1 cup buttermilk
- 1 tablespoon hot sauce
- 1 cup all-purpose flour
- 1 tablespoon paprika
- 1 teaspoon garlic powder
- 1 teaspoon cayenne pepper
- 1/2 teaspoon salt
- 1/2 teaspoon black pepper
- 1 cup vegetable oil (for frying)
- 3 tablespoons cayenne pepper
- 1 tablespoon brown sugar
- 1 teaspoon garlic powder
- 1 teaspoon paprika
- 1/4 teaspoon salt

Instructions:

1. Mix buttermilk and hot sauce in a bowl. Place chicken tenders in the mixture and marinate for at least 1 hour.
2. In another bowl, combine flour, paprika, garlic powder, cayenne pepper, salt, and pepper.
3. Heat vegetable oil in a frying pan over medium-high heat.
4. Dredge the chicken tenders in the seasoned flour mixture and fry for 5-7 minutes until golden and cooked through.
5. While the chicken cooks, mix cayenne, brown sugar, garlic powder, paprika, and salt in a bowl.
6. Once fried, toss the chicken tenders in the spicy seasoning mixture. Serve with pickles.

Spicy Smoked Sausage

Ingredients:

- 4 spicy smoked sausages
- 1 tablespoon olive oil
- 1/2 teaspoon smoked paprika
- 1/2 teaspoon cayenne pepper
- 1/2 teaspoon black pepper
- 1 teaspoon garlic powder
- 1 tablespoon hot sauce (optional)

Instructions:

1. Preheat your grill or smoker to medium-high heat.
2. Lightly oil the sausages and season with paprika, cayenne, black pepper, garlic powder, and hot sauce.
3. Grill the sausages for 5-6 minutes, turning occasionally, until fully cooked and lightly charred.
4. Remove from the grill and serve hot.

Chipotle Honey BBQ Chicken

Ingredients:

- 4 chicken breasts or thighs
- 1/4 cup BBQ sauce
- 1 tablespoon chipotle peppers in adobo sauce, chopped
- 2 tablespoons honey
- 1 tablespoon lime juice
- Salt and pepper to taste

Instructions:

1. Preheat the grill or oven to medium-high heat.
2. Mix BBQ sauce, chopped chipotle peppers, honey, lime juice, salt, and pepper in a bowl.
3. Coat the chicken with the sauce mixture and marinate for 30 minutes.
4. Grill the chicken for 6-7 minutes per side or bake in the oven at 375°F (190°C) for 25-30 minutes, until the chicken reaches an internal temperature of 165°F (74°C).
5. Serve hot, with extra sauce on the side.

Fiery BBQ Shrimp Boil

Ingredients:

- 1 lb shrimp, peeled and deveined
- 2 tablespoons olive oil
- 1 tablespoon Old Bay seasoning
- 1 teaspoon smoked paprika
- 1 teaspoon cayenne pepper
- 2 tablespoons hot sauce
- 1 lemon, sliced
- 4 ears of corn, cut into halves or thirds
- 1 lb baby potatoes
- 1/4 cup chopped fresh parsley

Instructions:

1. In a large pot, bring water to a boil and add potatoes and corn. Cook for 10 minutes.
2. Add shrimp to the pot and cook for another 3-4 minutes, until shrimp are pink and cooked through.
3. Drain the water and transfer the shrimp, potatoes, and corn to a large serving platter.
4. In a small bowl, mix olive oil, Old Bay, paprika, cayenne, and hot sauce. Drizzle over the shrimp and vegetables.
5. Garnish with lemon slices and parsley, and serve.

Spicy Dry Rub Baby Back Ribs

Ingredients:

- 2 racks baby back ribs
- 2 tablespoons olive oil
- 1 tablespoon smoked paprika
- 1 tablespoon brown sugar
- 1 teaspoon chili powder
- 1/2 teaspoon cayenne pepper
- 1/2 teaspoon ground black pepper
- 1 teaspoon garlic powder
- 1 teaspoon onion powder
- Salt to taste

Instructions:

1. Preheat your oven to 300°F (150°C).
2. Remove the membrane from the ribs and rub them with olive oil.
3. In a small bowl, combine all the dry ingredients, then rub them evenly over the ribs.
4. Wrap the ribs in aluminum foil and bake for 2.5-3 hours.
5. Unwrap the foil, brush the ribs with your favorite BBQ sauce, and bake for an additional 30 minutes.
6. Slice and serve hot.

Jalapeño BBQ Baked Beans

Ingredients:

- 2 cans baked beans
- 1 tablespoon olive oil
- 1 onion, chopped
- 2 jalapeños, seeds removed and finely chopped
- 2 tablespoons brown sugar
- 1/4 cup BBQ sauce
- 1 tablespoon apple cider vinegar
- 1/2 teaspoon smoked paprika

Instructions:

1. Preheat your oven to 350°F (175°C).
2. In a skillet, heat olive oil and sauté onions and jalapeños for 3-4 minutes until softened.
3. In a baking dish, combine baked beans, sautéed onions and jalapeños, brown sugar, BBQ sauce, apple cider vinegar, and smoked paprika.
4. Bake for 30 minutes, stirring halfway through.
5. Serve warm.

Spicy BBQ Meatballs

Ingredients:

- 1 lb ground beef
- 1 egg
- 1/2 cup breadcrumbs
- 1/4 cup grated Parmesan cheese
- 1 teaspoon garlic powder
- 1 teaspoon smoked paprika
- 1/2 teaspoon cayenne pepper
- 1/2 teaspoon ground black pepper
- 1 cup BBQ sauce
- 1 tablespoon hot sauce (optional)

Instructions:

1. Preheat your oven to 375°F (190°C).
2. In a bowl, combine ground beef, egg, breadcrumbs, Parmesan, garlic powder, paprika, cayenne, and black pepper. Mix until well combined.
3. Form the mixture into meatballs and place them on a baking sheet lined with parchment paper.
4. Bake for 18-20 minutes, until cooked through.
5. In a small saucepan, heat BBQ sauce and hot sauce (if using).
6. Toss the cooked meatballs in the sauce and serve hot.

Habanero BBQ Pulled Chicken

Ingredients:

- 4 chicken breasts
- 1 tablespoon olive oil
- 1 teaspoon garlic powder
- 1 teaspoon onion powder
- 1/2 teaspoon smoked paprika
- 1/2 teaspoon cayenne pepper
- 1/2 teaspoon ground black pepper
- 1 cup BBQ sauce
- 2 habanero peppers, finely chopped (seeds removed for less heat)
- 1 tablespoon honey
- 1 tablespoon apple cider vinegar

Instructions:

1. Preheat the oven to 375°F (190°C).
2. Heat olive oil in a large skillet over medium heat. Season chicken breasts with garlic powder, onion powder, smoked paprika, cayenne, black pepper, and salt.
3. Sear the chicken breasts on both sides until golden, about 4 minutes per side. Transfer to a baking dish.
4. In a small bowl, combine BBQ sauce, chopped habaneros, honey, and vinegar. Pour the sauce over the chicken.
5. Bake for 25-30 minutes, or until the chicken reaches an internal temperature of 165°F (74°C).
6. Shred the chicken with two forks, mixing it with the sauce, and serve hot.

Spicy Peach BBQ Pork Chops

Ingredients:

- 4 bone-in pork chops
- 1 tablespoon olive oil
- 1 teaspoon garlic powder
- 1 teaspoon smoked paprika
- 1/2 teaspoon cayenne pepper
- 1/2 teaspoon ground black pepper
- 1 cup peach preserves
- 1/4 cup BBQ sauce
- 1 tablespoon apple cider vinegar
- 1 tablespoon Dijon mustard

Instructions:

1. Preheat your grill to medium-high heat.
2. Season the pork chops with olive oil, garlic powder, paprika, cayenne, black pepper, and salt.
3. Grill the pork chops for 6-7 minutes per side, until cooked through (internal temperature should reach 145°F or 63°C).
4. In a saucepan, combine peach preserves, BBQ sauce, apple cider vinegar, and Dijon mustard. Simmer over low heat for 5 minutes.
5. Brush the sauce over the pork chops in the last few minutes of grilling. Serve with additional sauce on the side.

Southern Spicy BBQ Mac and Cheese

Ingredients:

- 1 lb elbow macaroni
- 2 tablespoons butter
- 1/4 cup all-purpose flour
- 2 cups milk
- 1 1/2 cups shredded cheddar cheese
- 1/2 cup shredded mozzarella cheese
- 1 teaspoon garlic powder
- 1/2 teaspoon smoked paprika
- 1 teaspoon cayenne pepper
- 1 cup BBQ sauce
- Salt and pepper to taste

Instructions:

1. Cook the elbow macaroni according to package instructions. Drain and set aside.
2. In a large saucepan, melt butter over medium heat. Whisk in flour and cook for 1-2 minutes.
3. Slowly add the milk while whisking to avoid lumps. Bring to a simmer until thickened.
4. Stir in the cheddar and mozzarella cheeses until melted and smooth. Season with garlic powder, smoked paprika, cayenne, salt, and pepper.
5. Mix the cooked pasta with the cheese sauce and add BBQ sauce to taste.
6. Serve hot as a creamy, spicy side dish or main.

Hot BBQ Burnt Ends

Ingredients:

- 2 lbs beef brisket, cut into cubes
- 2 tablespoons olive oil
- 1 tablespoon garlic powder
- 1 tablespoon onion powder
- 1 teaspoon smoked paprika
- 1 teaspoon cayenne pepper
- 1/2 teaspoon ground black pepper
- 1 cup BBQ sauce
- 1 tablespoon hot sauce (optional)

Instructions:

1. Preheat your smoker or grill to 250°F (121°C).
2. Season the brisket cubes with olive oil and the spice mix (garlic powder, onion powder, paprika, cayenne, black pepper).
3. Smoke the brisket for 3-4 hours, until tender and crispy on the outside.
4. Toss the burnt ends in BBQ sauce mixed with hot sauce (if using), then return to the smoker for an additional 30 minutes to set the sauce.
5. Serve the hot BBQ burnt ends with extra sauce.

Spicy Smoked Turkey Legs

Ingredients:

- 4 turkey legs
- 2 tablespoons olive oil
- 1 tablespoon smoked paprika
- 1 teaspoon garlic powder
- 1/2 teaspoon cayenne pepper
- 1 teaspoon ground black pepper
- 1 teaspoon ground thyme
- 1 cup BBQ sauce
- 1 tablespoon hot sauce (optional)

Instructions:

1. Preheat your smoker to 225°F (107°C).
2. Rub the turkey legs with olive oil, smoked paprika, garlic powder, cayenne, black pepper, and thyme.
3. Smoke the turkey legs for 3-4 hours, or until they reach an internal temperature of 165°F (74°C).
4. Brush with BBQ sauce mixed with hot sauce in the last 30 minutes of smoking.
5. Serve hot with extra BBQ sauce.

Cajun BBQ Catfish

Ingredients:

- 4 catfish fillets
- 2 tablespoons olive oil
- 1 tablespoon Cajun seasoning
- 1 teaspoon garlic powder
- 1/2 teaspoon smoked paprika
- 1/2 teaspoon cayenne pepper
- 1 tablespoon BBQ sauce
- 1 tablespoon lemon juice

Instructions:

1. Preheat your grill to medium-high heat.
2. Rub catfish fillets with olive oil and Cajun seasoning.
3. Grill the fillets for 4-5 minutes per side, until cooked through and flaky.
4. Brush with BBQ sauce mixed with lemon juice during the last minute of grilling.
5. Serve immediately with extra lemon wedges.

Spicy BBQ Beef Short Ribs

Ingredients:

- 4 beef short ribs
- 2 tablespoons olive oil
- 1 tablespoon chili powder
- 1 teaspoon garlic powder
- 1/2 teaspoon smoked paprika
- 1 teaspoon cayenne pepper
- 1/2 teaspoon ground black pepper
- 1/4 cup BBQ sauce
- 1 tablespoon hot sauce (optional)

Instructions:

1. Preheat your oven to 300°F (150°C).
2. Rub the short ribs with olive oil and season with chili powder, garlic powder, paprika, cayenne, black pepper, and salt.
3. Place the ribs on a baking sheet and cover with aluminum foil. Roast for 2.5-3 hours, until tender.
4. During the last 30 minutes, brush the ribs with BBQ sauce mixed with hot sauce.
5. Slice and serve with extra BBQ sauce.

Sweet and Spicy BBQ Cornbread

Ingredients:

- 1 box cornbread mix
- 1/2 cup milk
- 2 eggs
- 1/4 cup honey
- 1 tablespoon hot sauce
- 1/4 cup BBQ sauce
- 1/2 teaspoon cayenne pepper (optional for extra spice)
- 1/2 cup corn kernels (optional)

Instructions:

1. Preheat your oven to 375°F (190°C).
2. Prepare the cornbread mix according to package instructions, adding honey, hot sauce, and BBQ sauce.
3. Stir in cayenne pepper and corn kernels, if using.
4. Pour the batter into a greased baking pan and bake for 20-25 minutes, or until golden and a toothpick comes out clean.
5. Serve warm with extra BBQ sauce or honey.

Smoked Chicken with Spicy Rub

Ingredients:

- 4 bone-in chicken thighs
- 1 tablespoon olive oil
- 1 tablespoon chili powder
- 1 teaspoon garlic powder
- 1 teaspoon onion powder
- 1 teaspoon paprika
- 1/2 teaspoon cayenne pepper
- 1/2 teaspoon ground black pepper
- Salt to taste
- 1 cup BBQ sauce

Instructions:

1. Preheat your smoker to 225°F (107°C).
2. Rub the chicken thighs with olive oil, then season with chili powder, garlic powder, onion powder, paprika, cayenne, black pepper, and salt.
3. Smoke the chicken for 2-3 hours until the internal temperature reaches 165°F (74°C).
4. In the last 30 minutes of smoking, brush the chicken with BBQ sauce.
5. Serve the smoked chicken hot with additional BBQ sauce.

Spicy BBQ Pork Belly Bites

Ingredients:

- 2 lbs pork belly, cut into 1-inch cubes
- 1 tablespoon olive oil
- 1 tablespoon brown sugar
- 1 teaspoon chili powder
- 1 teaspoon garlic powder
- 1/2 teaspoon smoked paprika
- 1/2 teaspoon cayenne pepper
- 1/2 teaspoon black pepper
- 1/2 cup BBQ sauce
- 1 tablespoon hot sauce

Instructions:

1. Preheat the grill to medium heat.
2. Toss the pork belly cubes in olive oil, brown sugar, chili powder, garlic powder, paprika, cayenne, black pepper, and salt.
3. Grill the pork belly cubes for 10-12 minutes, turning occasionally until they are crispy on the outside and tender on the inside.
4. Mix BBQ sauce and hot sauce, then toss the cooked pork belly bites in the sauce before serving.

Ghost Pepper BBQ Sauce

Ingredients:

- 1 cup ketchup
- 1/4 cup apple cider vinegar
- 1/4 cup brown sugar
- 2 tablespoons Worcestershire sauce
- 1 tablespoon Dijon mustard
- 1 ghost pepper, finely chopped (handle with care)
- 1 tablespoon hot sauce (optional)
- 1 teaspoon garlic powder
- Salt and pepper to taste

Instructions:

1. In a saucepan, combine all ingredients and bring to a simmer over medium heat.
2. Stir frequently, and let the sauce cook for about 20 minutes to thicken and develop the flavors.
3. Taste and adjust the seasoning if necessary. Be cautious with the ghost pepper—it adds intense heat.
4. Let the sauce cool, then serve with your favorite grilled meats or as a dipping sauce.

Spicy Blackened Shrimp Tacos

Ingredients:

- 1 lb shrimp, peeled and deveined
- 1 tablespoon olive oil
- 1 teaspoon paprika
- 1/2 teaspoon garlic powder
- 1/2 teaspoon onion powder
- 1/2 teaspoon cayenne pepper
- 1 teaspoon ground cumin
- Salt and pepper to taste
- 8 small tortillas
- 1/2 cup coleslaw (optional)
- 1/4 cup sour cream
- 1 tablespoon lime juice
- Fresh cilantro for garnish

Instructions:

1. In a small bowl, mix the paprika, garlic powder, onion powder, cayenne, cumin, salt, and pepper.
2. Toss the shrimp with olive oil and coat evenly with the spice mixture.
3. Heat a skillet over medium-high heat and cook the shrimp for 2-3 minutes per side, until blackened and cooked through.
4. Warm the tortillas and assemble the tacos, adding the blackened shrimp, coleslaw, sour cream, and lime juice.
5. Garnish with fresh cilantro and serve.

Fiery BBQ Beef Burgers

Ingredients:

- 1 lb ground beef
- 1 tablespoon olive oil
- 1 tablespoon BBQ sauce
- 1 teaspoon garlic powder
- 1 teaspoon onion powder
- 1 teaspoon smoked paprika
- 1/2 teaspoon cayenne pepper
- Salt and pepper to taste
- 4 burger buns
- 4 slices pepper jack cheese
- 1/4 cup spicy BBQ sauce for serving

Instructions:

1. Preheat the grill to medium-high heat.
2. In a bowl, combine the ground beef with olive oil, BBQ sauce, garlic powder, onion powder, paprika, cayenne, salt, and pepper.
3. Form the mixture into 4 patties and grill for 5-6 minutes per side, or until the internal temperature reaches 160°F (71°C).
4. Add a slice of pepper jack cheese to each burger during the last minute of grilling.
5. Serve on buns with spicy BBQ sauce and your favorite toppings.

Spicy Grilled Corn with Cajun Butter

Ingredients:

- 4 ears of corn, husked
- 1/4 cup unsalted butter, melted
- 1 tablespoon Cajun seasoning
- 1/2 teaspoon garlic powder
- 1/2 teaspoon paprika
- 1/4 teaspoon cayenne pepper
- Salt and pepper to taste
- Fresh lime wedges for serving

Instructions:

1. Preheat the grill to medium heat.
2. In a bowl, combine melted butter, Cajun seasoning, garlic powder, paprika, cayenne, salt, and pepper.
3. Brush the corn with the seasoned butter and grill for 10-12 minutes, turning occasionally, until the corn is golden and slightly charred.
4. Serve with extra Cajun butter and lime wedges on the side.

Jalapeño Cheddar BBQ Sausages

Ingredients:

- 4 sausages (your choice of pork or beef)
- 1/4 cup diced jalapeños (seeds removed for less heat)
- 1/4 cup shredded cheddar cheese
- 1 tablespoon olive oil
- 1/2 teaspoon garlic powder
- 1 tablespoon BBQ sauce

Instructions:

1. Preheat the grill to medium-high heat.
2. Slice the sausages lengthwise and stuff them with diced jalapeños and shredded cheddar.
3. Drizzle the sausages with olive oil, sprinkle with garlic powder, and grill for 6-8 minutes per side until cooked through and crispy on the outside.
4. Brush with BBQ sauce during the last minute of grilling. Serve hot with extra cheese and jalapeños.

BBQ Brisket Nachos with Spicy Queso

Ingredients:

- 2 cups shredded BBQ brisket
- 1 bag tortilla chips
- 1 cup shredded cheddar cheese
- 1 cup shredded mozzarella cheese
- 1/4 cup sliced jalapeños
- 1/2 cup spicy queso (see below)
- 1 tablespoon sour cream
- Fresh cilantro for garnish

For Spicy Queso:

- 1 cup shredded cheddar cheese
- 1/2 cup milk
- 1 tablespoon jalapeño juice
- 1/4 teaspoon cayenne pepper

Instructions:

1. Preheat the oven to 375°F (190°C).
2. Spread tortilla chips on a baking sheet. Top with shredded BBQ brisket, cheddar and mozzarella cheeses, and sliced jalapeños.
3. Bake for 10 minutes or until the cheese is melted.
4. While the nachos bake, make the spicy queso by melting cheddar cheese with milk in a saucepan. Stir in jalapeño juice and cayenne pepper until smooth.
5. Drizzle the queso over the nachos and top with sour cream and fresh cilantro.

Carolina Hot Mustard BBQ Sauce

Ingredients:

- 1/2 cup yellow mustard
- 1/4 cup apple cider vinegar
- 1/4 cup honey
- 1/4 cup brown sugar
- 1 tablespoon Worcestershire sauce
- 1 teaspoon hot sauce
- 1/2 teaspoon cayenne pepper
- 1/4 teaspoon black pepper
- Salt to taste

Instructions:

1. In a saucepan, combine all ingredients and whisk to combine.
2. Bring to a simmer over medium heat, stirring frequently, and cook for 10-15 minutes.
3. Taste and adjust the seasoning with more salt, honey, or hot sauce as desired.
4. Let cool before serving with grilled meats or as a dipping sauce.

Spicy BBQ Pulled Beef

Ingredients:

- 3 lbs beef chuck roast
- 1 tablespoon olive oil
- 1 tablespoon chili powder
- 1 teaspoon smoked paprika
- 1 teaspoon garlic powder
- 1/2 teaspoon cayenne pepper
- Salt and black pepper to taste
- 1 cup BBQ sauce
- 1/4 cup beef broth
- 1 tablespoon hot sauce

Instructions:

1. Preheat the oven to 300°F (150°C).
2. Rub the beef roast with olive oil and season with chili powder, paprika, garlic powder, cayenne, salt, and black pepper.
3. In a large Dutch oven, sear the beef on all sides over medium-high heat for 3-4 minutes per side.
4. Add BBQ sauce, beef broth, and hot sauce to the pot. Cover and roast in the oven for 3-4 hours until the beef is tender and easily shredded.
5. Shred the beef using two forks and mix with the juices in the pot. Serve on buns or with your favorite sides.

Smoked Hot Link Sausages

Ingredients:

- 6 hot link sausages
- 1 tablespoon olive oil
- 1 tablespoon smoked paprika
- 1 teaspoon garlic powder
- 1 teaspoon onion powder
- 1/2 teaspoon cayenne pepper
- 1/4 teaspoon ground black pepper
- 1/2 cup BBQ sauce

Instructions:

1. Preheat the smoker to 225°F (107°C).
2. Rub the sausages with olive oil and season with smoked paprika, garlic powder, onion powder, cayenne, and black pepper.
3. Smoke the sausages for 1.5-2 hours, turning occasionally, until they are browned and cooked through.
4. In the final 10 minutes, brush the sausages with BBQ sauce and let it set.
5. Serve the hot links on buns or with a side of pickles.

Spicy BBQ Pork Ribs with Bourbon Glaze

Ingredients:

- 2 racks baby back ribs
- 1/4 cup brown sugar
- 1 tablespoon smoked paprika
- 1 teaspoon garlic powder
- 1 teaspoon onion powder
- 1/2 teaspoon cayenne pepper
- Salt and black pepper to taste
- 1/2 cup bourbon
- 1/2 cup BBQ sauce
- 1 tablespoon Dijon mustard

Instructions:

1. Preheat the grill to 275°F (135°C).
2. Remove the membrane from the ribs and rub them with brown sugar, smoked paprika, garlic powder, onion powder, cayenne, salt, and black pepper.
3. Grill the ribs indirectly for 2.5-3 hours, turning every 45 minutes.
4. While the ribs cook, make the bourbon glaze by simmering bourbon, BBQ sauce, and Dijon mustard in a saucepan over medium heat for 15 minutes.
5. In the last 15 minutes of cooking, brush the ribs with the bourbon glaze and grill until caramelized. Serve hot.

Sweet Heat BBQ Chicken Drumsticks

Ingredients:

- 8 chicken drumsticks
- 1 tablespoon olive oil
- 1 tablespoon brown sugar
- 1 teaspoon smoked paprika
- 1/2 teaspoon garlic powder
- 1/2 teaspoon onion powder
- 1 teaspoon cayenne pepper
- 1/2 cup BBQ sauce
- 1 tablespoon honey

Instructions:

1. Preheat the grill to medium-high heat.
2. Rub the chicken drumsticks with olive oil, brown sugar, smoked paprika, garlic powder, onion powder, cayenne, salt, and pepper.
3. Grill the drumsticks for 25-30 minutes, turning occasionally, until cooked through.
4. In the last 5 minutes of grilling, brush the drumsticks with BBQ sauce mixed with honey.
5. Serve hot with extra sauce for dipping.

BBQ Spicy Pickle Slaw

Ingredients:

- 2 cups shredded cabbage
- 1/2 cup shredded carrots
- 1/4 cup diced dill pickles
- 1/4 cup mayonnaise
- 2 tablespoons apple cider vinegar
- 1 tablespoon BBQ sauce
- 1 tablespoon hot sauce
- 1 teaspoon celery seeds
- Salt and black pepper to taste

Instructions:

1. In a large bowl, combine the shredded cabbage, carrots, and diced dill pickles.
2. In a separate small bowl, whisk together mayonnaise, apple cider vinegar, BBQ sauce, hot sauce, celery seeds, salt, and black pepper.
3. Pour the dressing over the cabbage mixture and toss to combine.
4. Chill in the refrigerator for at least 1 hour before serving.

Smoked Brisket Chili with BBQ Sauce

Ingredients:

- 2 lbs smoked brisket, shredded
- 1 tablespoon olive oil
- 1 onion, chopped
- 1 bell pepper, chopped
- 2 cloves garlic, minced
- 2 cups beef broth
- 1 can (14.5 oz) diced tomatoes
- 1 can (15 oz) kidney beans, drained and rinsed
- 1 can (15 oz) black beans, drained and rinsed
- 1/4 cup BBQ sauce
- 1 tablespoon chili powder
- 1/2 teaspoon cumin
- 1/4 teaspoon cayenne pepper
- Salt and black pepper to taste

Instructions:

1. Heat olive oil in a large pot over medium heat. Add onion, bell pepper, and garlic, cooking until softened.
2. Add the shredded smoked brisket and stir to combine.
3. Add beef broth, diced tomatoes, kidney beans, black beans, BBQ sauce, chili powder, cumin, cayenne, salt, and black pepper.
4. Simmer for 30 minutes, stirring occasionally, to allow the flavors to meld.
5. Serve hot, garnished with fresh cilantro or cheese if desired.

Spicy BBQ Meatloaf

Ingredients:

- 1 lb ground beef
- 1 lb ground pork
- 1/2 cup breadcrumbs
- 1/4 cup milk
- 1/4 cup BBQ sauce
- 1 egg
- 1/2 onion, chopped
- 2 cloves garlic, minced
- 1 teaspoon smoked paprika
- 1/2 teaspoon cayenne pepper
- Salt and black pepper to taste
- 1/4 cup hot sauce
- 1/4 cup BBQ sauce for glazing

Instructions:

1. Preheat the oven to 375°F (190°C).
2. In a large bowl, combine ground beef, ground pork, breadcrumbs, milk, BBQ sauce, egg, onion, garlic, smoked paprika, cayenne, salt, and pepper.
3. Shape the mixture into a loaf and place it on a lined baking sheet.
4. Mix hot sauce and BBQ sauce and brush over the top of the meatloaf.
5. Bake for 50-60 minutes until the meatloaf is cooked through and the internal temperature reaches 160°F (71°C). Serve hot.

Southern Spicy BBQ Deviled Eggs

Ingredients:

- 6 hard-boiled eggs, peeled and halved
- 1/4 cup mayonnaise
- 1 tablespoon Dijon mustard
- 1 tablespoon BBQ sauce
- 1 tablespoon hot sauce
- 1 teaspoon smoked paprika
- Salt and black pepper to taste
- 1/4 cup finely chopped pickles (optional)
- Fresh chives for garnish

Instructions:

1. Remove the yolks from the hard-boiled eggs and place them in a bowl.
2. Mash the yolks with mayonnaise, Dijon mustard, BBQ sauce, hot sauce, smoked paprika, salt, and black pepper until smooth.
3. Stir in the chopped pickles, if using.
4. Spoon the mixture back into the egg whites or pipe it for a more decorative look.
5. Garnish with fresh chives and serve chilled.

Habanero Honey BBQ Glazed Salmon

Ingredients:

- 4 salmon fillets
- 1/4 cup honey
- 2 tablespoons BBQ sauce
- 1 tablespoon habanero pepper sauce
- 1 tablespoon olive oil
- Salt and pepper to taste
- Fresh cilantro for garnish

Instructions:

1. Preheat the grill to medium heat.
2. In a small bowl, whisk together honey, BBQ sauce, habanero sauce, olive oil, salt, and pepper.
3. Brush the salmon fillets with the glaze and grill them for 4-5 minutes per side or until cooked to your desired doneness.
4. Once cooked, brush more of the glaze on top and garnish with fresh cilantro. Serve hot.

BBQ Cajun Shrimp and Grits

Ingredients:

- 1 lb shrimp, peeled and deveined
- 1 tablespoon olive oil
- 2 tablespoons Cajun seasoning
- 1/2 cup BBQ sauce
- 1 cup stone-ground grits
- 4 cups water
- 1/4 cup butter
- 1/4 cup grated Parmesan cheese
- Salt and pepper to taste
- Chopped green onions for garnish

Instructions:

1. Cook the grits by bringing water to a boil in a pot, then stirring in the grits. Reduce heat, cover, and simmer for 20-25 minutes until thickened. Stir in butter, Parmesan, salt, and pepper.
2. Heat olive oil in a skillet over medium-high heat. Toss shrimp in Cajun seasoning and cook for 2-3 minutes per side until pink.
3. Add BBQ sauce to the shrimp and stir to coat. Let it simmer for a minute to combine flavors.
4. Serve the shrimp over the grits and garnish with green onions.

Spicy BBQ Lamb Chops

Ingredients:

- 8 lamb chops
- 2 tablespoons olive oil
- 1 tablespoon smoked paprika
- 1 teaspoon cumin
- 1/2 teaspoon cayenne pepper
- Salt and black pepper to taste
- 1/2 cup BBQ sauce
- 1 tablespoon hot sauce

Instructions:

1. Preheat the grill to medium-high heat.
2. Rub the lamb chops with olive oil and season with paprika, cumin, cayenne, salt, and black pepper.
3. Grill the lamb chops for 4-5 minutes per side, or until desired doneness.
4. In the last few minutes of grilling, brush the chops with a mixture of BBQ sauce and hot sauce.
5. Serve the lamb chops hot, garnished with fresh herbs if desired.

Spicy Grilled Sweet Potatoes

Ingredients:

- 4 medium sweet potatoes, peeled and cut into rounds
- 2 tablespoons olive oil
- 1 teaspoon smoked paprika
- 1/2 teaspoon chili powder
- 1/4 teaspoon cayenne pepper
- Salt and black pepper to taste
- 1 tablespoon honey

Instructions:

1. Preheat the grill to medium heat.
2. Toss the sweet potato rounds with olive oil, paprika, chili powder, cayenne, salt, and black pepper.
3. Grill the sweet potatoes for 3-4 minutes per side until they are tender and have grill marks.
4. Drizzle the grilled sweet potatoes with honey before serving.

BBQ Pulled Pork Jalapeño Poppers

Ingredients:

- 12 large jalapeños, halved and seeded
- 1 cup cooked pulled pork
- 1/4 cup BBQ sauce
- 1 cup cream cheese, softened
- 1/2 cup shredded cheddar cheese
- 1/4 cup chopped green onions
- 1 tablespoon olive oil

Instructions:

1. Preheat the grill to medium heat.
2. Mix the pulled pork with BBQ sauce, cream cheese, cheddar cheese, and green onions.
3. Stuff the jalapeño halves with the pulled pork mixture.
4. Place the stuffed jalapeños on the grill and cook for 10-12 minutes until the peppers are tender and the cheese is melted.
5. Serve hot and enjoy.

Spicy BBQ Ribeye Steak

Ingredients:

- 2 ribeye steaks
- 1 tablespoon olive oil
- 1 tablespoon BBQ seasoning
- 1 teaspoon smoked paprika
- 1/2 teaspoon cayenne pepper
- Salt and black pepper to taste
- 1/4 cup BBQ sauce
- 1 tablespoon hot sauce

Instructions:

1. Preheat the grill to high heat.
2. Rub the ribeye steaks with olive oil, BBQ seasoning, smoked paprika, cayenne, salt, and black pepper.
3. Grill the steaks for 4-5 minutes per side, or until desired doneness.
4. In the last minute of grilling, brush the steaks with a mixture of BBQ sauce and hot sauce.
5. Let the steaks rest for a few minutes before serving.

Firecracker BBQ Sauce

Ingredients:

- 1 cup ketchup
- 1/4 cup apple cider vinegar
- 1/4 cup honey
- 2 tablespoons soy sauce
- 2 tablespoons Worcestershire sauce
- 1 tablespoon Dijon mustard
- 2 cloves garlic, minced
- 1 teaspoon smoked paprika
- 1 teaspoon cayenne pepper
- 1/2 teaspoon ground black pepper
- 1/4 teaspoon salt

Instructions:

1. In a saucepan, combine ketchup, vinegar, honey, soy sauce, Worcestershire sauce, mustard, garlic, paprika, cayenne, black pepper, and salt.
2. Bring to a simmer over medium heat, stirring occasionally.
3. Reduce heat and let it simmer for 10-15 minutes, allowing the flavors to meld together.
4. Remove from heat and let cool. Use as a dipping sauce or glaze for grilled meats.

Smoky Chipotle BBQ Chicken Thighs

Ingredients:

- 4 chicken thighs, bone-in and skin-on
- 1 tablespoon olive oil
- 2 tablespoons chipotle pepper in adobo sauce, chopped
- 1/4 cup BBQ sauce
- 1 tablespoon smoked paprika
- 1 teaspoon garlic powder
- Salt and black pepper to taste

Instructions:

1. Preheat the grill to medium heat.
2. In a small bowl, mix olive oil, chipotle pepper, BBQ sauce, smoked paprika, garlic powder, salt, and pepper.
3. Rub the chicken thighs with the marinade and let sit for 10-15 minutes.
4. Grill the chicken thighs for 7-8 minutes per side, or until the internal temperature reaches 165°F.
5. Brush with additional BBQ sauce during the last few minutes of grilling. Serve hot.

Spicy BBQ Bacon-Wrapped Jalapeños

Ingredients:

- 12 jalapeños, halved and seeded
- 6 slices bacon, cut in half
- 1/2 cup cream cheese, softened
- 1/4 cup shredded cheddar cheese
- 2 tablespoons BBQ sauce
- 1 teaspoon garlic powder
- Salt and pepper to taste

Instructions:

1. Preheat the grill to medium heat.
2. In a bowl, mix cream cheese, cheddar cheese, BBQ sauce, garlic powder, salt, and pepper.
3. Stuff each jalapeño half with the cream cheese mixture.
4. Wrap each stuffed jalapeño with half a slice of bacon and secure with toothpicks.
5. Grill for 8-10 minutes, turning occasionally, until the bacon is crispy and the jalapeños are tender. Serve hot.

Louisiana Spicy BBQ Shrimp

Ingredients:

- 1 lb shrimp, peeled and deveined
- 2 tablespoons olive oil
- 1 tablespoon Cajun seasoning
- 2 teaspoons smoked paprika
- 1/2 teaspoon cayenne pepper
- 1 tablespoon hot sauce
- 1/4 cup BBQ sauce
- 1 tablespoon lemon juice
- Salt to taste

Instructions:

1. Preheat the grill to medium-high heat.
2. In a bowl, toss shrimp with olive oil, Cajun seasoning, paprika, cayenne, hot sauce, BBQ sauce, and salt.
3. Skewer the shrimp and grill for 2-3 minutes per side until pink and cooked through.
4. Drizzle with lemon juice before serving. Serve with extra BBQ sauce if desired.

BBQ Chili-Lime Chicken Skewers

Ingredients:

- 2 chicken breasts, cut into bite-sized pieces
- 1 tablespoon olive oil
- 1 tablespoon BBQ seasoning
- 1 teaspoon chili powder
- 1 teaspoon cumin

- Zest and juice of 1 lime
- Salt and pepper to taste

Instructions:

1. Preheat the grill to medium heat.
2. In a bowl, combine olive oil, BBQ seasoning, chili powder, cumin, lime zest, lime juice, salt, and pepper.
3. Toss chicken pieces in the seasoning mixture and thread them onto skewers.
4. Grill the skewers for 4-5 minutes per side until the chicken is fully cooked and slightly charred.
5. Serve with lime wedges for extra flavor.

Hot BBQ Baked Beans with Andouille

Ingredients:

- 2 cans (15 oz each) baked beans
- 1/2 lb Andouille sausage, sliced
- 1 small onion, diced
- 1 tablespoon olive oil
- 1/4 cup BBQ sauce
- 1 tablespoon hot sauce
- 1 teaspoon smoked paprika
- 1/2 teaspoon garlic powder
- Salt and pepper to taste

Instructions:

1. Preheat the oven to 350°F.
2. In a skillet, heat olive oil over medium heat. Add sausage slices and cook until browned.
3. Add the diced onion and cook until softened, about 5 minutes.
4. In a baking dish, combine the baked beans, sausage mixture, BBQ sauce, hot sauce, smoked paprika, garlic powder, salt, and pepper.
5. Bake uncovered for 25-30 minutes, stirring occasionally. Serve hot.

Spicy BBQ Pimento Cheese Dip

Ingredients:

- 8 oz cream cheese, softened
- 1/2 cup mayonnaise
- 1/2 cup shredded sharp cheddar cheese
- 1/4 cup shredded Monterey Jack cheese
- 1/4 cup pimentos, drained and chopped
- 1 tablespoon hot sauce
- 1 teaspoon garlic powder
- 1/4 teaspoon cayenne pepper
- Salt and pepper to taste

Instructions:

1. In a bowl, combine cream cheese, mayonnaise, cheddar cheese, Monterey Jack cheese, pimentos, hot sauce, garlic powder, cayenne, salt, and pepper.
2. Mix until smooth and well combined.
3. Refrigerate for at least 1 hour before serving for best flavor.
4. Serve with chips, crackers, or vegetables for dipping.

www.ingramcontent.com/pod-product-compliance
Lightning Source LLC
LaVergne TN
LVHW081504060526
838201LV00056BA/2921